D1535694

FAQ

TEEN LIFE™

FREQUENTLY ASKED QUESTIONS ABOUT

Divorce

Rory M. Bergin
and Jared Meyer

ROSEN PUBLISHING®

New York

Published in 2012 by The Rosen Publishing Group, Inc.
29 East 21st Street, New York, NY 10010

Library of Congress Cataloging-in-Publication Data

Bergin, Rory M.
Frequently asked questions about divorce / Rory M. Bergin,
Jared Meyer.—1st ed.
    p. cm.—(FAQ, teen life)
Includes bibliographical references and index.
ISBN 978-1-4488-4632-0 (library binding)
1. Children of divorced parents—Juvenile literature.
2. Divorce—Juvenile literature. 3. Divorced parents—
Juvenile literature. I. Meyer, Jared. II. Title.
HQ777.5.B473 2012
306.89—dc22

2010048418

Manufactured in the United States of America

CPSIA Compliance Information: Batch #S11YA: For further information, contact Rosen Publishing, New York, New York,
at 1-800-237-9932.

Contents

WHAT HAPPENS WHEN A FAMILY DIVORCES?

A divorce is the legal end of a marriage. Over the past several years, millions of people in the United States have faced divorce. Statistics indicate varying rates of divorce. The most commonly cited statistic indicates that one in every four families will face divorce. Divorce occurs often, and it can happen to anyone. People decide to seek divorce for many reasons. No two family situations are exactly the same.

If your parents have decided to divorce, you will likely experience all kinds of feelings and think all kinds of thoughts. You may be worried about how your life will be affected or how often you may see your parents. Or you may experience anxiety and awkwardness about having a relatively new routine, living with only one parent at a time. You might want to talk over your concerns with someone. Maybe

A couple meets with a lawyer to discuss the divorce process.

you want to ask someone for answers to your questions or just want to share your concerns with someone you think will understand.

Often teens find it difficult to share their feelings openly, and you might also. Maybe you are too embarrassed or think no one will understand your feelings. You may know that divorce happens to other families but may not have thought it would ever happen to yours. You might wonder how your life could be turned upside down so quickly and why there does not seem to be anything that you can do about it. Most of all, you may be wondering how and why this could happen.

The Effects on Teens When Parents Fight

Teens often see that their parents are clearly not getting along but might hold on to the hope that they will work out their differences. No one likes the fighting between two parents, and some children may be hurt by the instability and uncertainty of their lives. Worse even than the fighting and the anger, however, is the thought of one's parents actually breaking up.

You might react to your situation in one way, but someone else might react in quite another. If the fighting and hostility between your parents grow, so may your sense of discontentment with the family's situation. A home should be a place of shelter, love, and security. These qualities may no longer be available to someone whose parents aren't getting along very well. The lack of these essential ingredients for a stable home life can affect the entire household.

It is extremely difficult for teens to witness long-term fighting and hostility between parents, the two people on whom they rely to provide their most basic needs and sense of stability, security, and comfort. During this time in your life, you are likely to be going through tremendous physiological, social, and emotional changes independent of whatever your parents are experiencing. You may be experiencing the growing pains of puberty and adolescence, engaging in the normal and natural changes of this stage of your development.

You may choose to distance yourself from your parents and family situation by spending more time with friends who will accept you and make you feel that you belong. You may begin to stay out late at night, not letting your parents know where you are going or when you may return. You may want to be independent and run your own life. You may be suffering but may not know how to effectively deal with your pain. For a long time you may suffer in silence when your parents argue. The months and years of witnessing hostility between parents can harden a person, but they do not erase one's yearning for closeness and belonging.

When Divorce Comes as a Surprise

More than one million people have parents who separate or divorce each year. The decision to separate can happen quite suddenly in some families, causing shock and dismay and leaving teenagers totally unprepared to cope. When divorce occurs suddenly and without apparent warning in a family, teens naturally wonder what will happen to them and whether their lives will ever be normal again.

The fear of the unknown is common to nearly all people. A lot of us fear change, and divorce brings many major changes to one's relationships and daily life. When news of a divorce arrives as a sudden announcement, it can be a profound shock and may produce an immediate feeling of uncertainty and a lack of confidence and hope for the future.

The fear of change may grip you so tightly that you may begin to fall apart in many ways. You may find yourself unwilling or unable to talk to either of your parents or confide in anyone at school. Your situation may be so overwhelming to you

Hearing the news that your parents are divorcing can be an enormous shock. Sadness, depression, and anger may all result, but you will all survive this difficult time.

that you find it difficult to study or take part in any of your normal activities. You may lose interest in the things that had been most important to you before and that had seemed such a natural part of your personality. Your grades could drop, and you may no longer associate with old friends. Sadness, fear, and loneliness could seem to take over completely.

Whether someone is somewhat prepared for their parents' separation or totally surprised by it when it is announced, all children of divorce have a couple of important things in common. They will all be deeply affected by what is happening in their families, and their responses will be completely natural and understandable under the circumstances. This is not the same thing as saying that there are only a few ways to respond to such news or that all the pain teens experience will be absolutely inevitable. Nor is it justification to act out one's anger and fear in destructive or antisocial ways. But it is an acknowledgement that divorce represents a profound family crisis, and the anger, fear, uncertainty, and sadness it engenders will affect teens strongly. Especially in the first months after a divorce, teens need to seek and receive help by talking about their feelings with friends, family members, and therapists. They should seek and receive good coping strategies from this support network.

The Blame Game

Divorce is a painful experience for everyone involved. This includes both of the parents and the children. If your parents have divorced, you know how hurt and confused you can become. Suddenly living with only one parent can fill you with all kinds of unhappy feelings. You will naturally miss your absent parent. You may also feel some guilt about the divorce. You may think that you could have prevented it. You couldn't have. You may think that you caused it somehow. You didn't.

You might also be very angry with both of your parents. You may blame them for splitting up your family. These feelings are natural. And they will take time to get over. During a divorce you need to talk to both of your parents about your feelings and fears. By telling them how you really feel, you can get in better touch with your emotions and increase your self-knowledge and self-awareness. Additionally, you can help your family understand how you feel and how that affects your behavior. Talking with a counselor will also help you express your feelings in a productive way. All of this will help you feel more in control of yourself during a confusing and chaotic time.

People involved in a painful situation such as a divorce look for someone to blame. If your parents have just divorced, they may be blaming each other. How should you feel when this happens? A divorce can happen for any number of reasons. You might not understand all of the reasons, but you can try to accept what has happened to your family.

A divorce is not only one person's fault, so you should try not to blame anyone. You may want to blame one of your parents for the divorce. But remember, a marriage takes two people. And so does a divorce. If you're still experiencing anger long after the divorce, you may need help handling your feelings. You can talk with a counselor at school or at your place of worship.

It is important for parents to stress to their child that the divorce is not his or her fault and there was nothing he or she could have done better or differently to change the outcome.

Seeking to lay blame for a divorce is normal, but often people find that it doesn't help. It only forces you to think about the negative aspects of the situation. It doesn't help you get on with your life. Parents get a divorce because of their own problems, not because of something the children have said or done. Many children think that they have somehow caused their parents' divorce. This guilt makes children angry and depressed. They may turn to drugs to escape. Some may even attempt suicide. These teens feel guilty about something that was beyond their control.

If you ever feel that something you did caused your parents to divorce, tell your parents your thoughts right away. They may not be aware of your feelings. They can reassure you that their divorce was not your fault. A divorce is something that occurs between two parents—not between parents and their children.

Suddenly Living in a Single-Parent Family

Many single-parent families are created when a married couple divorces. A divorce legally ends a marriage. Husband and wife find separate places to live. Usually the children of a divorced couple live with one of the parents either full-time (sole physical custody) or most of the time (joint physical custody). Typically, the other parent in a joint custody arrangement may have the children on alternate weekends, part of the summer vacation, and some holidays. The parent that has sole or primary custody of the children is the main person responsible for caring for them. When children begin living with the parent who has sole or primary custody, they become part of a single-parent family.

Families that go through a divorce often find their world turned upside down. A divorce changes more than your living situation. It can also affect how much money the family has to live on and where you go to school. All of these are drastic changes, and they often occur within a very short period of time. If your family is going through a divorce and starting a single-parent home, there will be a lot to get used to. Although it's going to be very difficult, if you can accept the changes in your life over time and learn how to deal with them, you may find that you'll be happier.

One challenging outcome of divorce is that the parent with custody of the children may have more trouble making ends meet on a single income, even with child support payments from the other parent.

Your parents' divorce and all the changes it brings will upset you. Tell your parents how you feel. It may be hard to talk to both of them at the same time. But it's important that they both know how their divorce makes you feel. If you talk about your feelings, you will be able to adjust more easily to all the changes going on around you. Expressing yourself will help you feel more comfortable in your new single-parent situation. A counselor or a close friend can give you good tips on how to start this kind of conversation and support you in your coping efforts.

WHAT IS THE GRIEVING PROCESS?

Separation or divorce causes grief to many people, both young and old, similar to any other profound loss. After all, it is a kind of death—the death of a central relationship within the family. Any reaction to such loss includes a set of specific emotional responses and behaviors that together constitute what psychologists, therapists, and social workers sometimes call the stages of grief. In this view, grief is not a single, distinct emotion but a process of working through several emotions associated with loss. For teenagers, the divorce of their parents can be one of the most profound losses they can experience.

Denial: "This Isn't Really Happening"

When you first realize that your parents are going to separate or divorce, your immediate response might be

Sadness, regret, and denial are all common reactions to the divorce of one's parents, but so, too, are eventual acceptance and a renewed commitment to a happy future.

disbelief. You might not want to believe it, or you might wish that it would not happen. You might go around telling yourself that you do not really care, that it does not matter one way or the other, or that you are not going to show anyone how much it hurts. Denial is a way of easing the pain that you are feeling and insulating yourself from it. It is our way of protect-

ing ourselves from what we believe will be a painful experience. Denial works to a certain extent. However, when denial prevents you from reaching any of the other stages, even more serious problems can result.

Many people regard carrying on in the face of a divorce, as if nothing has happened, as brave or courageous. In many ways, moving on in this way is indeed brave and courageous. However, when such behavior prevents you from accessing all your feelings about the loss or accepting its reality, even greater long-term problems can result. For example, some people who don't express themselves naturally when they are young may express behavioral problems as adults because they don't learn how to freely express their emotions verbally.

Anger: "I'll Show Them"

When you experience an emotional shock, anger is a common response. You may get mad because you feel like a victim. Victims feel helpless because bad things have happened to them that they did not cause and cannot fix. Everyone likes to feel that they have control over their life and feel outraged, infuriated, and scared when they realize they don't. You may be angry because you know that your life and family will change drastically. In the beginning stages of the divorce, you may not be sure what this change will mean in your life. The following are typical ways that children of divorce express their anger:

- Not eating
- Acting rebellious
- Not sleeping well
- Changing study habits
- Hanging out with a new crowd, often people who are bad influences or whom your parents don't approve of
- Experimenting with tobacco, alcohol, and drugs

Sorrow: "Everything Has Changed"

Sadness is a natural response to learning that your parents are splitting up. The underlying causes for your feelings are easy to understand. For example, you may recognize that your relationship

Some teens react to the stress, uncertainty, sadness, and anger churned up by their parents' divorce by engaging in self-destructive activities, or "acting out." Abusing alcohol and drugs is one common form of acting out.

with your parents will be different. You may know that you will have to leave one parent to live with another. You may feel sorry for your parents, too, because you care about them and you know that what they are going through is also making them very sad. You may even sense that your life will never be the same again, and that thought may make you very unhappy and unsettled. It is important to be honest with yourself about these feelings. They are quite normal. If you do not face them, they will find a resting place somewhere within you and, sometime in the future, may interfere with healthy emotional responses to other situations.

Fear: "What Happens Next?"

If you know that you have to go someplace that you have never been before, and you have heard nothing but bad things about it, it is understandable that you might be afraid. It is much the same with learning that your parents are separating. In a way, the news means that you will be going somewhere that you have never been, and everyone has certainly heard a lot of negative things about life after divorce.

It is very common to fear the unknown, and fear of the unknown can be more terrifying than actually experiencing it. Fear is a normal and natural response during the early stages of a family's breakup. Your parents may be scared, too. Sensing their fear can cause you to feel even more insecure. When you are able to face this feeling and tell others how you feel, you will find that it is not as difficult as you might have thought. You will learn that others have had similar feelings and experiences. You will learn how they managed to cope with those feelings.

Life after divorce can change so completely, so quickly, that it is both disorienting and frightening. Soon, however, new routines and ongoing relationships with your parents will create a renewed sense of stability and familiarity.

Blame: "Who's Fault Is It?"

When something bad happens, it is natural to look for an explanation. It is unsettling to think that things can just happen and that there is sometimes little or nothing that you can do about it. You might look for a reason for your parents' divorce and, sometimes, someone to blame.

If the divorce is sudden, the parent who leaves is the one who is usually blamed. In the case of longstanding arguments, complaints, and bickering, you may continuously shift blame from one parent to the other and back again. Children and teens often

> In the early days of a divorce, there can suddenly feel like there is no chance for future happiness. With time, acceptance, and adjustment, however, peace, contentment, and optimism will again enter your life.

blame themselves for the divorce. Sometimes, even though they know that they did not cause the marital problems, they can blame themselves for not being able to stop it from happening.

Acceptance: "We're Going to Move On and Be OK"

At last, if a teen is able to work through these feelings and stages of grief, he or she will reach the stage of acceptance. At this point, teens have resigned themselves to the fact that their parents are splitting up. There is no definite time period for each of these stages. Some teens will stay in the denial stage longer than others will. Some may reach the acceptance stage before others. The point here is to understand that all of these feelings and stages of grief are part of a normal process of getting through an enormously difficult period in your life.

Myths and Facts

Myth **Teens are sometimes partially or entirely the reason for their parents' divorce.**

Fact ➡ A teen's attitude or behavior is never the specific cause of his or her parents' divorce. Adults get divorced because their relationship is irreparable based on their chemistry, compatibility, communication styles, and long-term life goals.

Myth **People who quickly jump into relationships and get married are as likely to quickly jump out of them.**

Fact ➡ While not taking a substantial amount of time to develop the foundation needed for healthy and enduring marriage is a risk to the long-term prospects of a relationship, many people who marry soon after meeting and dating nevertheless remain together for the rest of their lives. Conversely, many people who date and live together for a long time before marrying often divorce within years of the wedding. The amount of time spent dating before marriage is only one variable in the complicated equation of what makes a marriage succeed or fail.

 Parents who have experienced failed marriages are considered to be "damaged goods" or to have "lots of baggage." Fact ➡ While divorce has some stigmas attached to it and some people do leave marriages scarred by unhappiness, guilt, and/or emotional suffering, many go on to begin new and healthy relationships, often with others who also were once married and understand how difficult both marriage and divorce can be.

three

WHAT HAPPENS IF I'M CAUGHT IN THE MIDDLE?

If your parents separate or divorce, you might find yourself in an extremely awkward position. You have, up to that point, likely shared your love and loyalty more or less equally between both parents. Divorce can force you to feel like your loyalties are divided or are being tested, which can result in a new set of conflicting feelings and emotions.

It can be difficult for you to remain loyal to both parents. When your parents are together, you may feel a sense of balance, togetherness, and unity. You may have the sense that everyone feels the same way about each other. Yet in the wake of a divorce, you might find yourself siding with the parent to whom you feel closer or the parent that you feel has been wronged in the process. If you take sides, however, another conflict can develop in the form of

It is extremely important to spend quality time with both parents after a divorce. The parent-child relationship must be nourished in order for it to remain strong and sustaining.

guilt about favoring one parent over the other. When this happens, you may blame one or both parents for the guilt and conflicted feelings you are experiencing.

Determining Custody

In a divorce, there is another element of taking sides that often affects teenagers. Unless the parents are able to reach an agreement themselves on all the elements of the divorce, outside professionals often become involved. These can include lawyers, judges, therapists, psychologists, social workers, and other mediators and health care professionals. Dealing with your feelings by yourself is difficult enough; being asked to share them with strangers and outsiders can be very awkward and painful.

The most common situation in which you may have direct contact with such professionals is if your parents cannot agree on who will have custody of you. Custody is often thought of as determining with which parent the teenager will live. This is known as physical custody. Physical custody and day-to-day parental care is only one part of the custodial equation, however. It also involves the legal responsibility for raising and providing for the teen and making decisions about the child's welfare. This is known as legal custody. If one parent is given sole physical custody, generally the other has visitation rights. Sometimes parents agree to joint physical and legal custody.

When divorcing parents cannot agree on who will have physical and legal custody of the children, a family court judge often makes the decision for them. Custody is often the most contentious issue in a divorce case. In deciding which parent is to be given custody, judges often try to determine what would be in the best interest of the child. However, in most states, there is no law that establishes specific standards or guidelines that judges must follow in deciding such cases.

For many years, the feeling was that the mother was the best parent to be assigned the responsibility for raising the children, unless she was proven to be negligent or abusive in the past. The assumption was that the mother's primary role was that of nurturer and caregiver, while the father was the primary financial

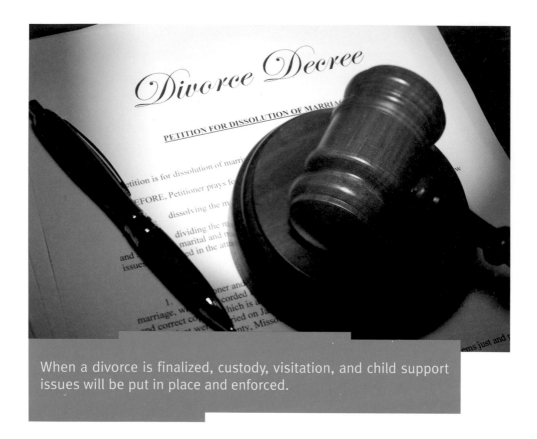

When a divorce is finalized, custody, visitation, and child support issues will be put in place and enforced.

supporter of the family. Thus, the most common outcome of custody disputes was that the mother would be assigned custody of children and the father would be assigned to pay the mother a certain percentage of his income for child support. Although this is still the most common outcome, in the last two decades an increasing number of fathers have received physical custody. Joint custody, in which parents share both the day-to-day and legal responsibilities, has also become much more common.

Do you have to take sides when your parents are fighting about custody issues? Emotionally, it is often difficult not to. Yet the thought of being forced to express a preference for one parent over another, either privately or in a public forum like a courtroom, is often agonizing. However, it is rare that a teenager, especially a younger teen, would be made to testify in court, in front of a judge, about which parent he or she would prefer to live with. What is more likely to happen is that a professional assigned by the court—usually a psychologist, therapist, or social worker—will interview the teen about his or her home life and feelings about the situation and then issue a report to the court. The judge considers the recommendations found in such reports when arriving at a custody decision.

In such situations, teenagers may feel less like they are taking sides than that they are being torn apart emotionally by love for and loyalty to both parents. It is important that teens find someone to help them deal with their emotions. Ideally, this should not be a professional appointed by a court or someone who is working on behalf of one of the parents in the custody matter. What teens need is an independent therapist or counselor whose only interest is what is best for them, which is not always what is best for the parents.

Moving Out

Interestingly, more divorced fathers are beginning to raise children alone after a divorce. Sometimes when parents begin to have marital difficulties, the mother leaves first. This usually adds to the teen's stress over the family's breakup. Traditionally, the mother is the one who provides the glue that binds the

Sometimes divorce also means a move to a new home, town, or even state. This can be upsetting, but try to stay positive and embrace the new experiences that you are about to have.

family together. Legally, this is reflected in the presumption that, in most cases, the mother is the one who should have custody. However, certain circumstances dictate the hard choices that parents sometimes make. The father plays just as important a role in the family as the mother does, so when a father leaves, it is equally difficult on the rest of the family. Regardless of who leaves and who has primary day-to-day custody, as long as teens have a secure home headed by a responsible, supportive, and caring parent, they will most likely be assured of healthy development.

It is normal for you to want your parents to stay together. You may even attempt to delay, or stall, the process in the hope that your parents will stay together. Young adults have different ways of directly or indirectly trying to let their parents know how they feel. Many teenagers have common concerns when their parents are separating or divorcing, such as wondering whether or not they will be able to survive financially with only one working parent, if they will have to move to a smaller house or apartment, or whether they will have to move to a new town or even a new state. These are concerns that are commonly felt during the early stages of the divorce process. During this stage, when your feelings are still very new and intense and you are not quite sure how to deal with them, it is important to talk over your thoughts and feelings with someone—a friend, family member, school counselor, or professional therapist.

Getting Caught in the Middle

It is awkward and agonizing to be caught in the middle of your parents' separation. Adolescents choose a variety of ways to stay out of this no-win position. Some parents help their teens avoid getting caught in the middle by shielding them from their own conflicts as much as possible. For some parents, however, the divorce process is overwhelming and disorienting, and without knowing it or meaning to, they drag their children into the conflict.

Parents use various tactics to engage their children in the conflict. Some parents unwittingly seek their help to support them in the conflict. Sometimes they use their teens to gain information about the activities of the other spouse. These tactics can prove extremely harmful to teens in the long run and make the early stage of the divorce or separation process even more difficult for them.

You may find yourself squarely in the middle of your parents' problems. You may want to help, as teens often do in such situations. When you find out that you cannot fix their marriage, however, you may blame yourself rather than realizing that only your parents can solve their problems. In response, you may withdraw and rebel.

Perhaps when you were a child, your parents' arguments made you afraid. As a teenager, you may feel anger and resentment toward them. Yet a part of you may feel that you can still help them and mend their relationship. You may get involved in their arguments, trying to understand why your parents are not able to get along. You could talk to your parents separately, but your efforts to mediate their conflict may bring you too close to their disagreements. Ultimately, this may only make their separation more difficult for you to accept. You have to learn how to separate yourself from your parents' conflicts, without separating from your parents.

In emotional terms, teens may choose to get out of the middle by withdrawing from both parents totally. Although it is understandable, in many ways this may not be the best decision for them. They may become disconnected from their parents and lost within themselves. They may be unable to resolve any of the inner conflicts that they feel over the breakup of their family.

Avoid getting caught in the middle of your parents' divorce. It is not your responsibility to referee their arguments or mend their relationship.

They need to find a way to remain connected to both parents but disconnected from their conflict.

Sometimes teens take on the responsibility of trying to help their parents work things out. This, of course, produces more anxiety and stress and keeps them squarely in the middle of their parents' conflict. It is not the teen's responsibility to counsel one or both parents, side with one parent against the other, or attempt to bring the two parents back together and mend their marital relationship. Parents divorce or separate for their own reasons, and they must work through and resolve the con-flict in their own way.

When the normal flow and structure of the family breaks down, adolescents often attempt to take on adult responsibili-ties. Although it is admirable to act as grown up as possible in any situation, teens are not adults, and they should not expect themselves to resolve, handle, or deal with adult problems. Very few adults handle divorce well, so teens should not be surprised if they find themselves overwhelmed at times and not coping as well as they would like. Being forgiving of and patient with one-self is crucial when dealing with the divorce of one's parents. Doing the best you can under very difficult circumstances is a great achievement in itself.

four

HOW CAN I ADJUST TO THESE CHANGES?

There is no denying that divorce can be an extremely difficult experience in a variety of ways. In its different stages, it can cause many complications. However, the initial period of shock and confusion does pass, and loving relationships between family members can and do resume. These relationships will be different in some ways than before, but different does not always mean worse. In some ways and in certain circumstances, divorce can actually make family relationships better. Family members can be forced by the disruption of divorce to become more mindful and aware of their interactions with each other and work harder to strengthen their relationships.

This does not happen automatically, of course. It requires understanding, acceptance of the new way of life that will emerge, and careful communication among family members. In some cases, this kind of communication is a skill that family members need to learn, both individually and together. In the best case, you may begin to understand some of the positive outcomes of the breakup. You may learn to see each of your parents in a very different light. Though you may have learned to view them for the most part as a team, you may now get to know them as individuals. With some resolution of the problems that separated them, your parents may have more energy and time to put into their relationship with you.

You can draw new meanings from your relationship with each parent. Your life may actually become more stable without some of the conflicts that were present in the final stages of your parents' marriage and the early stages of divorce or separation. The past is a permanent part of you, but now you welcome the present, and it is beginning to feel OK. Your brighter future beckons.

Keeping the Lines of Communication Open

Families experiencing divorce may learn that communicating openly and honestly is the key to calming their fears and easing the burdens of their changing lifestyle. Through honest communication, you may be able to better understand some of the reasons why your parents chose to separate. Until you are able to talk to your parents about what is happening to them, you can only guess what is going to happen to your family, and this wondering and guessing can cause inner conflict, confusion, anxiety, and uncertainty.

If you had to move after your parents' divorce, you may be the new kid in a new school. Hard as this is, just trust that new friendships will develop over time and soon this new environment will feel as familiar as your old school.

Adjusting to the Newness of Everything

Adjusting to your new life will have its high moments and its low moments. You may have to adjust to many new things: a new relationship with your parents, a new home, a new school, new friends, and a new community, for instance. Though you may stay in the same home, there is also the chance that you will move. You may have to say good-bye to old friends and have to find new ways to maintain those friendships while trying to make new ones. You will also be learning to adjust to new relationships in your parents' lives if they begin dating other people. The latter is probably one of the most difficult adjustments of all.

Staying Close with an Absent Parent

Even though your parents' custody arrangement may separate you physically from one of your parents, the separation does not necessarily have to interfere with the parental influence that your parent had and will continue to have in your development. That parent might, in fact, become an even stronger influence in your life. You and your parent may learn to place an even greater value on the time you have together.

It may take added effort on the part of your absent parent and you to develop and maintain this closeness, but the effort is worth it. When this happens, you may begin to seek the advice of the absent parent in positive ways. Keep in mind that some teens use the absent parent to challenge the advice or directions of the custodial parent. In effect, they play one parent against the other in order to get what they want or simply to create con-flict and passively express their anger over the divorce. These are negative ways to respond to the situation and can prolong the postdivorce adjustment period.

You will probably spend more time alone, without either of your parents. A single parent will have a little less time, perhaps, to spread between work, home, and parental responsibilities. You will need to develop a more responsible attitude and become more independent, which are things you would probably want to be working on anyway. Within just a few years you will graduate

Suddenly being part of a one-parent household means you may spend a lot more time alone. This can provide valuable opportunities for processing what has happened and what comes next.

high school and probably be out of the house, so developing independence and resourcefulness now is a great advantage.

Maintaining Old Friendships in Your New Life

Your parents' divorce may mean that you have to move away from your town or state. This change in your life will have an impact on your friendships. When divorce necessitates a move to another town or city, it means that you will be saying good-bye to old friends. However, this does not mean that you have

Nowadays it's easier than ever to stay in touch with friends in other towns, states, or even countries via Internet communications like Skype, e-mail, texts, tweets, and instant messages.

to say good-bye to the friendships. You may only be moving across town or to a neighboring town. Even if you are moving far away, you may be seeing each other on your visits back home with the other parent, and you might find ways to communicate through letters or by e-mail, text, instant message, tweet, telephone, or Skype. If your friendships are important to you, you will find a way to maintain them by keeping up with the news about what is going on in each other's worlds.

When Your Parents Begin Dating Other People

Adjusting to a one-parent family is a challenge in itself, but you may also be faced with an even bigger challenge: your parents dating other people. Most people do remarry after divorce. If your parents do start to see other people, or perhaps even decide to remarry, you might face many different emotional challenges. First and foremost, it may be a challenge to stay out of the middle of the developing relationship.

It is natural to look for comparisons between this new individual and your other parent. On the other hand, liking this person too much might place you in that uncomfortable middle position again and make you feel disloyal to your other parent. Your one parent might question you about the dating activities of the other parent. This may place more of a burden on you as you struggle with this new life, but in time, you will learn to adjust to these new relationships.

Remarriage and Blended Families

A blended family, or stepfamily, is a family that is formed by one or two partners who have been married before and who may have children from their previous marriages. The parent's new spouse becomes a stepparent if the parent has children from his or her first marriage. Blended families can be made up of stepsiblings, blood siblings (including new children your parent and stepparent may have together), and various sets of birth and stepparents. You personally may have your blood siblings, your stepsiblings, and your stepparent all living together in your household.

According to the Stepfamily Association of America, 65 percent of second marriages involve children from previous marriages. This means that numerous blended families have formed, and perhaps you are a member of one of them, or even two of them if both of your natural parents have remarried. Fifty-two to 62 percent of all first marriages will eventually end in legal divorce. Similarly, 60 percent of all remarriages eventually end in legal divorce, so there are many blended families out

Blended families are quickly becoming the norm in North America. They offer their members an enlarged and loving network of support, friendship, and strong family ties, which can be a great balm after the trauma of divorce.

there. About 43 percent of all marriages are remarriages for at least one of the married people, and more than half of Americans today have been, are, or will be in one or more step-family situations.

If you hear that one of your parents is getting remarried, you may have many different emotions. You might be upset that your parent is marrying someone else. You may be angry and think that this new person is trying to take the place of your absent parent. Perhaps you are an only child who is living alone with a single parent, and you fear that your stepparent will ruin

Though the notion of suddenly being asked to live with a new step-parent and stepsiblings may be initially alarming, it very often turns out to be a rare new opportunity for love, laughter, understanding, and close companionship.

that special, close relationship you have with your natural parent. In any case, it can be very difficult for a teenager to watch a parent enter into a marriage with someone new.

One out of every three Americans is now a stepparent, a stepchild, a stepsibling, or some other member of a stepfamily. Learning to be part of a blended family is often a challenge. There are many children who must learn to cope with the complexities of blended family life, but for a teenager, it may be especially difficult to adjust to that life. You may be going through so many changes already, and you may be starting to gain your independence and seek your own identity. These changes are complicated by having to adapt to the dynamics of a new family. You may be wondering where you fit in the new scheme of things at home.

With the formation of new family units, stepparents and stepsiblings may play new roles in your life. You may experience a variety of feelings regarding your new family. You may be angry or sad, or you may be excited about the new situation. Or you may not have feelings one way or the other. If your natural parents are divorced or you have experienced the death of a parent, you may have all kinds of emotions and concerns about suddenly acquiring new parents and new siblings.

On the other hand, you may have positive feelings about the remarriage. Your stepsiblings and stepparent may become great companions, friends, and sources of love and support. Even though remarriage is a change, it doesn't have to be a bad thing.

HOW CAN I SEEK RESOLUTION, HEALING, AND GROWTH?

Important lessons can be learned from divorce. You may learn about conflict and how to resolve it. You might learn how to maintain relationships through love, caring, and support of one another. You may even learn about forgiveness. Teens learn that life goes on. They learn that even if their parents date and marry other people and introduce stepsiblings into the family, their parents' love for them will continue. Teens may find that they can adjust to the new people in their parents' and their own lives.

Divorce may teach you about attachments and the true meaning of family. When members of a family separate, it is important that the parents continue to be involved in the lives of their teens. If parents continue to maintain family ties, teens will not only survive the divorce, but

Seeking professional counseling can be enormously helpful for couples, parents and children, and individuals. Therapists and counselors can help resolve disagreements within families and address the inner conflicts that beset the individual.

they may in fact thrive. And in the process, they will learn valuable lessons about the things that are truly important in life.

Conflict Resolution

Conflict is a part of life. Sometimes conflict can be resolved without much difficulty. Other times much effort will be required in order to reach a resolution. Some conflict will not be resolved. However, it is always advantageous to try to resolve conflict, and almost any attempt to resolve it is beneficial. Through these attempts, individuals can learn about themselves and come to a better understanding of those with whom they're arguing.

Unresolved conflict between people can lead to deeper problems and greater personal dissatisfaction in the long term. Some people attempt to ease these negative interpersonal feelings through unhealthy means such as alcohol or other substances and other types of self-destructive behavior.

Conflict resolution is a skill that can be learned. Many professionals teach conflict resolution. Marriage counselors and therapists can teach conflict resolution strategies to couples who are experiencing marital problems, contemplating divorce, or already in the midst of divorce proceedings. These skills and strategies can be useful whether people are working on their marriage or coping with the aftermath of the relationship's end. Another type of professional, a divorce mediator, helps settle conflicts that arise from the division of property or custody issues.

People find many ways to resolve conflict. There are simple steps that you can follow, however, that facilitate this process. The first step is laying the cards on the table. In this stage, each person in the conflict presents his or her view of the situation. The key is that each person agrees to listen to the other's point of view about the problem without interruption. What you are trying to do is understand the other person's thinking while giving him or her the chance to understand your own. This step lays the groundwork for an eventual agreement, resolution, and reconciliation.

The next step is finding common ground. In this stage, you are trying to find some point, no matter how small, upon which the two of you can agree. You both have to agree to accept some

Open and honest communication, though initially daunting, helps ensure a solid and enduring relationship between a parent and child. Mutual listening, sharing, and understanding are the keys to a respectful, loving, and lasting relationship.

degree of mutual responsibility for the conflict or problem and look for areas of compromise.

The third step is commitment. After you both have laid your cards on the table and found some common ground, you are then ready to look for points of agreement that will lead to a renewed commitment to the relationship and its maintenance. Hopefully, after these steps are taken, you will be able to commit to taking actions that will resolve the disagreement or dispute and prevent future occurrences. One additional benefit to this type of counseling is that any lessons learned about resolving conflict can be applied to future relationships, helping to increase the chances for a more successful outcome.

A Hard-Won Maturity and Wisdom

Teens who have experienced the separation or divorce of their parents often show increased maturity in many ways. This maturity may stem from discovering that family security, stability, and happiness are not guaranteed and should never be taken for granted. They may have also discovered that love, by itself, is not always enough to ward off disagreement and conflict.

Children of divorce watched as their parents struggled with themselves and with each other in their attempts to smooth the wrinkles in their lives. As their parents formed new relationships and new family groupings, they had to make adjustments that other teens did not. Teens of divorced parents must adjust not only to changes in their relationships with their parents, but also to the changes in their own friendships. Finally, in the process, teens often learn the important lesson of forgiveness.

Let It Go

Forgiveness is important because it allows you to get rid of anger. Anger is a very destructive and toxic emotion, causing individuals to make poor, regrettable choices. It is bad enough to witness or live in an environment filled with stress and conflict. But holding on to anger and resentment only prolongs these feelings and prevents healing from taking place.

Divorce does hurt, but those involved can learn many lessons from the experience. Perhaps the most important one is that they can overcome the hurt and disappointment, and they can find a new way of life.

Getting Help

When you are in the middle of the messiness of your parents' separation and divorce, you probably will not be quite sure how you're supposed to feel or even what you are actually feeling at any particular time. But there are ways that you can gain a better understanding of these feelings. During this time, you need support.

The first step toward healing is to seek understanding of your situation. You will need help with this; you cannot do it alone. Sometimes this help can come directly from your parents. However, in the early stages of their separation they may be too overwhelmed and unable or unavailable to help you as much as you would like. This is the time to seek other resources.

Your first thought might be to talk to a relative or a friend. However, it is essential that you seek out people who can be objective and neutral about the situation. Family members, for example, might find it hard to be objective because they are involved to some extent and may feel more loyalty to one or the other parent. There are others who will be able to listen more objectively and provide knowledgeable support.

Guidance Counselors

You might think of your school guidance counselors only as your source of information and advice regarding college and career planning. However, another important aspect of their work is personal counseling. Counselors often organize discussion or support groups for students with similar experiences and problems, or they can put you in touch with such groups. They have

Do not hesitate to lean upon your school's guidance counselors or therapists when you are having a hard time coping with the strains of family life. They know how to help and can offer invaluable insights and coping strategies.

been trained in how to provide support to students who may be facing any number of problems, including divorce and its aftermath.

Social Workers and Psychologists

A school psychologist and a school social worker are probably in your school full-time or on a periodic basis, maybe two or three times each week. Both are available to help you understand your feelings. They will be able to help you determine what feelings are typical in your situation and when and whether you may need to seek further professional help.

Librarians

There have been many books and articles written on the various aspects of divorce that can help teens and younger children cope with their changing family situation. Your school librarian is a valuable resource who can help you find material on the subject. Your public library will also have a wide variety of self-help titles on divorce. These books can help you find the necessary support for understanding your circumstances.

A Long and Winding Road Toward Greater Insight and Wisdom

Eventually, you will likely reach the point of acceptance of your parents' divorce. If you do, you will know that you and your family will survive. You will learn to trust that your parents made the best decision possible for all concerned. From then on it will be easier for you to accept that, though your life will be different, it can still be shared with both of your parents. Finally, by experiencing the changing nature of relationships, teens are exposed to valuable lessons about what to expect when they are confronted with conflict or choice in their own relationships. At the end of this long and difficult process, do not be surprised if you begin to see yourself differently. This means that you have learned something about yourself, others, and family relationships and what it takes to make them succeed, grow, and evolve.

Ten Great Questions
to Ask Your Therapist

1 What are the reasons my parents are ending their marriage?

2 What is the best way that all of us can move on with the least amount of conflict or drama?

3 What can I do to make this difficult time easier for my parents?

4 If I'll be living with both parents, is it possible to live with each of them every other week?

5 What will the house rules in each of my parent's homes be like now that we're no longer one big family?

6 If I'll be living in two homes, will I have clothing and personal stuff in each home?

7 Do I have any say in the decision about which parent I will live with?

8 How will my parents' divorce affect my perception of relationships, commitment, and conflict?

9 How will my parents' breakup affect my life compared to my friends whose parents are still together?

10 Is it possible that my parents will get back together again sometime in the future? Should I encourage a reconciliation or try to bring them back together?

Glossary

acting out Responding to unresolved stress or inner conflict by behaving in harmful, destructive, or uncharacteristic ways.

conflict resolution The process of finding solutions to a dispute that minimize the destructive consequences of the disagreement and are mutually satisfactory to both parties.

custody Literally, immediate supervision and control. In the context of divorce, custody refers to which parent is assigned the legal responsibility for raising the children of the marriage.

denial In psychology, a defense mechanism whereby a person deals with a situation that is causing stress or conflict by denying the existence or reality of the situation.

depression A psychological condition characterized by prolonged feelings of sadness, hopelessness, worthlessness, or despair.

divorce The legal termination of a marriage.

grief Long-lasting or deep distress, most often caused by a death or profound loss.

marriage The legal and/or religious union of two individuals.

mediator A neutral party who assists in negotiations and conflict resolution.

physiological Pertaining to the healthy or normal functioning of an organism.

psychologist Clinical professional who works with patients in a variety of therapeutic contexts, including counseling.

resolution The act of solving a problem or dispute or determining a solution that is mutually agreeable.

social worker A professional who helps people overcome problems and make their lives better. Through their research and practice, they seek to improve the quality of life and further the development of the potential of each individual, group, and community of a society. Social workers perform interventions through research, policy, community organizing, direct practice, and teaching.

surrogate A substitute.

therapist A person trained in methods of treatment and rehabilitation other than the use of drugs or surgery, especially in treatment of emotional or psychological issues.

Action Alliance for Children (AAC)

1201 Martin Luther King Jr. Way

Oakland, CA 94612

(510) 444-7136

Web site: http://www.4children.org

The AAC works to inform, educate, connect, and inspire
people who work with and on behalf of children.
It provides useful, reader-friendly information on
current issues, trends, and public policies that affect
children and families, for families, early care and
education staff, people who work with them,
and advocates.

American Academy of Child and Adolescent
Psychiatry (AACAP)

3615 Wisconsin Avenue NW

Washington, DC 20016-3007

(202) 966-7300

Web site: http://www.aacap.org

The AACAP is the leading national professional medical
association dedicated to treating and improving the
quality of life for children, adolescents, and families
affected by mental, emotional, behavioral, and develop-
mental disorders.

American Association for Marriage and Family Therapy (AAMFT)
112 South Alfred Street
Alexandria, VA 22314
(703) 838-9808
Web site: http://www.aamft.org
Since its founding in 1942, the AAMFT has been involved
with the problems, needs, and changing patterns of couples
and family relationships. The association leads the way to
increasing understanding, research, and education in the
field of marriage and family therapy.

Chadwick Center for Children and Families
3020 Children's Way, MC 5016
San Diego, CA 92123
(858) 576-1700, ext. 4249
Web site: http://www.chadwickcenter.org
The Chadwick Center promotes the health and well-being of
at-risk children and their families. It accomplishes this
through excellence and leadership in evaluation, treatment,
prevention, education, advocacy, and research.

Children's Rights
330 Seventh Avenue, 4th Floor
New York, NY 10001
(212) 683-2210
Web site: http://www.childrensrights.org
Children's Rights is a national advocacy group working to
enshrine in the law of the land every child's right to grow
up in a safe, stable, permanent home.

Child Welfare League of America (CWLA)

1726 M Street NW, Suite 500

Washington DC, 20036

(202) 833-1638

Web site: http://www.cwla.org

This powerful coalition of private and public agencies has been
serving vulnerable children and families since 1920. Its
expertise, leadership, and innovation on policies, programs,
and practices help improve the lives of millions of children
in all fifty states and worldwide.

Divorce Source, Inc.

P.O. Box 1580

Allentown, PA 18105-1580

(610) 820-8120

Web site: http://www.divorcesupport.com

The Divorce Support Web site provides divorce information on
family law topics such as divorce, child custody, visitation,
child support, alimony, and property division.

International Bureau for Children's Rights (IBCR)

2715 Chemin de la Côte-Sainte-Catherine

Montréal, QC H3T 1B6

Canada

(514) 932-7656

Web site: http://www.ibcr.org/eng/home.html

The IBCR is an international nongovernmental organization
(INGO) based in Montreal, Canada. The IBCR's mission
is to contribute to the promotion and respect of the

Convention on the Rights of the Child adopted by the United Nations in 1989 and now ratified by 192 countries.

Kids' Turn
55 New Montgomery, Suite 500
San Francisco, CA 94105
(415) 777-9977
Web site: http://kidsturn.org
Kids' Turn is a nonprofit organization that helps children understand and cope with the loss, anger, and fear that often accompany separation or divorce. It awakens parents to the need to support their children during this crisis in their lives so that at-risk behavior by children is averted.

New Beginnings
558 Castle Pines Parkway, Unit B-4 #364
Castle Rock, CO 80108
(303) 706-9424
Web site: http://www.newbeginningscoparenting.com
New Beginnings has been informing and educating people with its coparenting after divorce classes since 1995.

Rainbows Canada
80 Bradford Street, Suite 545
Barrie, ON L4N 6S7
Canada
(877) 403-2733
Web site: http://www.rainbows.ca

Rainbows Canada is an international, not-for-profit organization that fosters emotional healing among children grieving a loss from a life-altering crisis. These losses, among others, include separation, divorce, death, incarceration, and foster care.

Voices for America's Children
1000 Vermont Avenue NW, Suite 700
Washington, DC 20005
(202) 289-0777
Web site: http://www.voices.org
Voices for America's Children is the nation's largest network of multi-issue child advocacy organizations. This nation-wide, nonpartisan, nonprofit network leads advocacy efforts at the community, state, and federal levels to improve the lives of all children, especially those most vulnerable, and their families.

Web Sites

Due to the changing nature of Internet links, Rosen Publishing has developed an online list of Web sites related to the subject of this book. This site is updated regularly. Please use this link to access the list:

http://www.rosenlinks.com/faq/div

For Further Reading

Amos, Janine. *Divorce*. New York, NY: Windmill Books, 2009.

Brotherton, Marcus. *Split: A Graphic Reality Check for Teens Dealing with Divorce*. Sisters, OR: Multnomah Publishers, 2006.

Casella-Kapusinski, Lynn. *Now What Do I Do?: A Guide to Help Teenagers with Their Parents' Separation or Divorce*. Skokie, IL: ACTA Publications, 2006.

Danziger, Paula. *The Divorce Express*. New York, NY: Puffin, 2007.

Deal, Ron L. *The Smart Step-Family: Seven Steps to a Healthy Family*. Ada, MI: Bethany House, 2006.

Ford, Melanie, et al. *My Parents Are Divorced Too: A Book for Kids by Kids*. 2nd edition. Washington, DC: Magination Press, 2006.

Gates, Elizabeth. *Dealing with Divorce: Finding Direction When Your Parents Split Up*. Grand Rapids, MI: Zondervan, 2008.

Howell, Maria L. *Divorce and Children*. Farmington Hills, MI: Greenhaven, 2009.

Mattern, Joanne. *Divorce* (The Real Deal). Portsmouth, NH: Heinemann Educational Books, 2008.

McDowell, Josh, and Ed Stewart. *My Friend Is Struggling with Divorce of Parents*. Ross-shire, Scotland: CF4K, 2009.

Murphy, Patricia J. *Divorce and Separation*. Heinemann
    Educational Books, 2007.
Schab, Lisa M. *The Divorce Workbook for Teens: Activities to
    Help You Move Beyond the Breakup*. Oakland, CA: Instant
    Help Books, 2008.
Sindell, Max. *The Bright Side: Surviving Your Parents' Divorce*.
    Deerfield Beach, FL: Health Communications, 2007.
Smith, Krista. *The Big D: Divorce Thru the Eyes of a Teen:
    Student Workbook*. Scottsdale, AZ: AMFM Press, 2010.
Trueit, Trudi Strain. *Surviving Divorce: Teens Talk About
    What Hurts and What Helps*. New York, NY: Franklin
    Watts, 2007.

About the Authors

Rory M. Bergin is a writer who lives in New Rochelle, New York.

Jared Meyer is a speaker, author, and marketing specialist who has written several books for Rosen about educational and social strategies for success in the teen years.

Photo Credits

Cover © Tom McCarthy/PhotoEdit; p. 5 Pixland/Thinkstock; p. 8 Jupiterimages/Brand X Pictures/Thinkstock; p. 11 Buccina Studios/Photodisc/Thinkstock; p. 13 Keith Brofsky/Valueline/Thinkstock; pp. 15, 20, 26, 35, 37 Shutterstock.com; p. 17 © www.istockphoto.com/Stockphoto4u; p. 24 Comstock/Thinkstock; p. 19 Liquidlibrary/Thinkstock; p. 28 © Michael Newman/PhotoEdit; p. 31 iStockphoto/Thinkstock; pp. 38–39 © David Young-Wolff/PhotoEdit; p. 41 Digital Vision/Thinkstock; p. 42 Nick White/Digital Vision/Thinkstock; p. 45 © www.istockphoto.com/Josh Rinehults; p. 47 Jupiterimages/Creatas/Thinkstock; p. 50 © Dennis MacDonald/PhotoEdit.

Designer: Evelyn Horowicz; Photo Researcher: Peter Tomlinson